Henry Hitchcock

American State Constitutions

A Studie of their Growth

Henry Hitchcock

American State Constitutions
A Studie of their Growth

ISBN/EAN: 9783742811851

Manufactured in Europe, USA, Canada, Australia, Japa

Cover: Foto ©ninafisch / pixelio.de

Manufactured and distributed by brebook publishing software
(www.brebook.com)

Henry Hitchcock

American State Constitutions

QUESTIONS OF THE DAY.—XXXVII

AMERICAN
STATE CONSTITUTIONS

A STUDY OF THEIR GROWTH

BY

HENRY HITCHCOCK, LL.D.

NEW YORK AND LONDON

G. P. PUTNAM'S SONS

The Knickerbocker Press

1887

COPYRIGHT BY
G. P. PUTNAM'S SONS
1887

Press of
G. P. PUTNAM'S SONS
New York

AMERICAN STATE CONSTITUTIONS.*

Mr. President and Gentlemen of the Association:

That saying of Andrew Fletcher, of Saltoun, two centuries ago, is still sometimes quoted : " That if a man were permitted to make all the ballads, he need not care who should make the laws of a nation."

Whether this be not an extravagant statement, we need not now inquire. It may be conceded that the ballads, still more the folk-songs of higher degree, which find a permanent foothold in the traditions and the literature of a people, must leave their mark upon its character and even upon its institutions. Yet the name —*Chansons de Geste*, songs of action, or of what has been acted—given to such poems as the Spanish Song of the Cid, and its French parallel in subject and form, the Song of Roland, implies that the deeds of valor and the scenes of pathos whose memory they made immortal were the flower and the fruit of a national life already existing. They are an expression of that life, rather than the mould in which it was formed. So the ballad of Chevy Chase, which Sir Philip Sidney said "stirred his blood like the sound of

---

* An address delivered before the N. Y. State Bar Association at its tenth annual meeting, at Albany, N. Y., January 18, 1887.

trumpet," did not create, though it commemorated, the
feuds of the Border and the fierce conflicts of Percy and
Douglas. If the song of Harmodius and Aristogeiton,
handed down through the centuries before Christ, in-
spired the youth of Athens to resist tyrants, as Theodore
Körner's " Lyre and Sword," only seventy years ago,
inflamed his comrades of the Free Corps to still more
daring exploits, it was because the former met with eager
response in the Greek love of liberty, the latter in the
German love of Fatherland.

But whatever may be the significance or the influence
of the songs of a people, it is certain that in the laws
under which they live we shall find, explicitly or implicitly, the fullest expression of their national life. Those
laws tell us, explicitly, what conceptions of right practically obtain among them, in what methods and by what
machinery those conceptions are enforced. Implicitly
they contain, and to the patient student they reveal, the
past as well as the present life of the society in which
they prevail ; for laws and constitutions are a growth,
not a manufacture. Theorists and doctrinaires may con-
struct,—as has been said of the Abbé Sieyes (Carlyle's
" Constitution Builder "),—a new constitution for every
day in the year. Philosophers like John Locke may
elaborate them from classic models for infant colonies.
Imperial charlatans, posing as saviors of society, may for
a time cajole or compel even an intelligent and patriotic
people to accept their edicts. But neither constitutions
nor laws nor institutions have ever permanently endured
among a people whose national life was real and not

stagnant, except in so far as they did express and reflect that life.

"*Naturam expellas furca, tamen usque recurret.*"

I am sure that you will agree with me that the implicit record of a people's history, past and present, which may be read between the lines of its formal legislation, is a deeply interesting one. The statute of 43d Elizabeth, recognized in many of our States to-day as the basis of their law of charitable trusts—what a kindly light it sheds upon the humane and philanthropic impulses of modern civilization! What a history of benefactions its brief preamble contains! How lavish and varied the endowments which it tersely recites as then existing in England, for the relief of poverty and suffering, the maintenance of disabled public servants, the promotion of learning, even the relief or redemption of prisoners and captives,—a description of charity which became less urgent some two hundred years later, when American pluck led the way in the suppression of Algerine piracy. The immediate purpose of that statute was simply the reformation of alleged abuses in administering those charities, by the appointment of commissioners to inquire into and prevent the same. But if, as a law in force, its life was short, it survives as a witness to the charity of our forefathers ; as the footprints upon fossil-bearing rocks reveal to the geologist the species and even the habits of birds and animals long since extinct. So Bishop Stubbs, in his great work on the Constitutional History of England, has drawn from English statutes of the fourteenth to the sixteenth centuries important testimony

as to the condition of laborers, the combination of arti-
sans for enforcing higher wages,—topics not unknown to
our own times,—and the organization of those merchant-
guilds and craft-guilds or companies, whose growth indi-
cated the decay of the feudal military system and the
advent of modern industrial civilization.

Turn to the first constitution of your own State of New
York, adopted April 20, 1777, amid the din of the first
conflicts of the War of Independence, by a Convention
which assembled on July 10, 1776.   Its preamble contains a brief but fervid denunciation of " the many tyran-
nical and oppressive usurpations of the King and Parlia-
ment of Great Britain on the rights and liberties of the
people of the American colonies," and is ablaze with the
spirit which before long made Saratoga famous by the
surrender of Burgoyne.   It sets forth at large the Declaration of Independence adopted at Philadelphia but a few
days before your Convention assembled at White Plains,
and the unanimous resolve of the latter body on July 9,
1776: " That the reasons assigned by the Continental
Congress for declaring the United Colonies free and
independent States are cogent and conclusive."   This
was writing history, as well as enacting an organic law.
No provision is found in that instrument looking to surrender or even to a possible reconciliation of the colonies
with Great Britain.   On the contrary, besides establishing
a government for the new State, it provides for a census of
its inhabitants to be taken seven years subsequent to the
termination of the war, and also, for " a fair experiment
to be made," by legislative enactment after the war

should have ended, whether the substitution of the ballot for the *viva-voce* method of voting then in use "would tend more to preserve the liberty and equal freedom of the people." One is reminded of the Romans, who continued, it is said, at the same prices as before, to buy and sell lands within their city while the Gauls were thundering at its gates. So swift had been the march of events, so rapidly had become impassable the gulf between the former loyal subjects of Great Britain and its Crown since the 2d day of July, 1776,—when a similar Convention in New Jersey, while declaring, in the State constitution which it adopted on that day, that all civil authority under the king of Great Britain was necessarily at an end, nevertheless added, as its final clause, a proviso in the following words:

" Provided always, and it is the true intent and meaning of this Congress, that if a reconciliation between Great Britain and these Colonies should take place, and the latter be taken again under the protection and government of the crown of Britain, this charter shall be null and void, otherwise to remain firm and inviolable."

But it is needless to multiply illustrations of the deeper significance of statutes and constitutions. Every student of history has learned from his Shakespeare and his Scott as well as from Gibbon and Macaulay, that when illuminated by genius they become instinct with life and meaning—as the slender filament of dry carbon glows in the electric lamp.

But while the laws of a people—using that term in its widest sense—at the same time express its national life and implicitly record its history, it is also true that they exert a powerful, often a controlling, influence upon the direction and the measure in which that life shall be developed. The promulgation of the Mosaic code among the Hebrews, the compilation of the laws of Menu by the Brahmins, the adoption of the code of Solon and of the laws of Lycurgus in Greece and of the Twelve Tables at Rome, are familiar illustrations of this truth, which the chronicles of all ages confirm.

Nowhere is this more impressively stated than by Sir Henry Maine, in the first chapter of his well-known work on Ancient Law. That learned writer, tracing the development of primitive law after its embodiment into a code, points out that thenceforward what may be called its spontaneous development ceases; that the changes thereafter effected in it are effected deliberately and from without; and that from the moment when their laws are thus embodied in some permanent record, the stationary condition of the human race is the rule, the progressive the exception. His discussion of the changes which took place in primitive law, after the era of codes, is confined to the "progressive societies." Concerning these he makes a general statement of great importance, which is best given in his own words:

"With respect to them [progressive societies] it may be laid down that social necessities and social opinion are always more or less in advance of Law. We may come indefinitely near to the closing of the gap between them, but it has a perpetual tendency to reopen. Law is stable; the societies we are speaking of are progressive. The greater or less happiness of a people depends on the degree of promptitude with which the gulf is narrowed."

I need not remind you with what learning and ability Sir Henry Maine has illustrated and developed this important truth in its application to Ancient Law, nor of his well-known statement of the agencies—Legal Fictions, Equity, Legislation—by which Law is brought into harmony with society. I have referred to the passage just quoted, because it is applicable to every progressive society, at every stage of its existence ; and because the observations which I venture to submit to you to-day relate to some of the phenomena which illustrate its application to the society in which we live.

I desire very briefly to call your attention to a few of the more important changes which the people of the several States of this Union have made, from time to time, especially during the past generation, in the more permanent portion of the laws which govern them,— changes in the constitutions of those States, as distinguished from their current statutory legislation.

Let me say at once, however, that I have no thought of attempting either an elaborate statement or an adequate discussion of those changes. Only to enumerate them would take more time than even your good-nature could spare. To expound them aright, to make plain their true significance, would be a task demanding the genius and training of the true publicist, together with ample opportunity and leisure for the patient comparative study through which alone that can be discovered. What I have proposed to myself is simply to

remind you of some few of the more important enactments of this character, grouping them for convenient
reference, and to suggest some inquiries which seem
to me not without interest, and which in competent
hands might be profitably followed up.

Such changes as these, whether in the form of amendments or in that of new or revised constitutions, may be
regarded in more than one aspect. Considered as part of
the organic law, they are new declarations by the people
of the respective States, acting in their sovereign capacity
under the sanctions of law provided for authenticating
such action, as to what shall thereafter constitute absolute
rules of action and decision for all departments and officers of the government, in respect of the matters therein
mentioned, and subject to the limitations contained in
the Constitution of the United States.

But these constitutional enactments are also social and
political phenomena. We may study them in order to
learn, not only what they prescribe, but, so to speak,
what they reveal. As such phenomena they have,—not
only for the student of historical jurisprudence but for
every thoughtful man, concerned for the future of his
country,—a significance quite distinct from that which
they have either for the officer who must execute, or for
the citizen who must obey them. They are *res gestae* in
a far more important sense than were the cries of the
mob, admitted as competent evidence on the trial of
Lord George Gordon. They signify and express, not the
            civium ardor, prava jubentium,
but the conclusions of a free people as to what changes

in their organic law will best promote the common welfare. Wise or unwise, wholesome or dangerous, those conclusions reveal, in some measure at least, the drift of that people's thought, the goal to which, consciously or unconsciously, it is tending; as Agassiz demonstrated from the sluggish flow of the Mer de Glace past the stakes which he had planted at its former verge, not only that the huge glacier was a slowly moving river of ice, but also the rate and direction of its irresistible drift into the valley beneath.

Such enactments are to be classed among those materials out of which, as Mr. Buckle has said, a philosophic history can alone be constructed. They form indeed but a very small part of the vast aggregate of facts, with which the future historian must deal—a very small part even of the legislation of the several societies which have adopted them, and whose vigorous life is expressed and recorded from day to day in a thousand other ways.

But they are unique in their importance, as being the broadest, the most permanent, the most authoritative expression of that life. They are the very foundations of the accepted political and social order ; they mark out the chosen lines of progress ; they record, in brief but weighty phrase, the results of controversies the most momentous. Three lines sufficed for that declaration in the Thirteenth Amendment to the Constitution of the United States, after the promulgation of which African slavery ceased to have any legal sanction.

But however valuable they are as material for the historian, the question of their true significance is of

vastly greater interest to the people themselves, whose
future, for good or evil, they forebode. It is of peculiar
interest to the people of this country, most of all to our
own profession, since each one of us must share the re-
sponsibility, as well as the results, of the great experiment
of Democracy in these United States. I say "experiment," in no doubting or fearful sense. The life of every
free man, of every free people, must be an experiment
until it is ended, just because they are free to choose
between good and evil, though powerless to escape the
inevitable consequences of their final choice. May I
recall those grave and earnest words with which De
Tocqueville concludes his work on " Democracy in
America ":

" The nations of our time cannot prevent the conditions of
men from becoming equal ; but it depends upon themselves
whether the principle of equality is to lead them to servitude
or freedom, to knowledge or barbarism, to prosperity or to
wretchedness."

There have been prophets not a few, as we all know,
some of whom have doubted, others have denied, the
more fortunate of these alternatives. Philosophers and
statesmen have echoed the gloomy prediction of the historian, Macaulay, thirty years ago, that it would be im-
possible to establish permanent institutions based upon
universal suffrage, and have repeated with ominous shake
of the head the scornful phrases in which Carlyle de-
scribed the struggle to preserve our Union, and warned
us that we were, or soon would be, " shooting Niagara."
With some, no doubt, the wish was father to the thought.

But it is hardly worth one's while to argue with prophets,
—whether, from across your Canadian border, they predict
a continent submerged by tidal waves at the next con-
junction of that undiscovered planet, Vulcan, or from
beyond the ocean they foretell a republic dismembered
among the breakers of anarchy and civil strife. It was
Fisher Ames, I believe, who compared a monarchy to a
gallant ship, all sails set and colors flying, but suddenly
wrecked upon hidden rocks ; and a republic to a raft, the
people on which have their feet in the water most of the
time, but the raft never goes down. After all, these
predictions are best answered by the logic of events. It
is our business to take care of the logic by controlling the
events. As the motto of George Washington had it :
Exitus acta probat. That steadfast, patient, and cheerful
faith in the strength and permanence of a government
of the people, by the people, for the people, which is the
birthright of every American, is founded upon eternal
principles of justice and equal right, whose ultimate
prevalence and vindication are as much a part of the
order of the universe as are the movements of the planets
in their spheres. The conditions of righteousness which
they impose are indeed inexorable for nations as for individual men. That those conditions, like the Sibyl's price
to Tarquin, will sooner or later be exacted in full, we
have learned from the bitter experience of that struggle
for the Union, that irrepressible conflict, so long, so often,
so vainly postponed. But we also learned even from the
agony of that conflict, that the institutions thus brought
into deadly peril by our own default had borne fruit in.

that great and typical American, whose patient and unflinching faithfulness to duty, whose marvellously clear and kindly insight, whose large-hearted wisdom, born of wide experience and deep sympathy with the plain people from among whom he sprung, made him a true leader of men ; at whose untimely death the universal cry of grief from our own land was echoed by every civilized people, and whose name is more illustrious, his immortal memory more beloved, with every passing year. And we remember that after that struggle was past, after the disbanded armies, North and South, had returned to the pursuits of peace, and the republic had entered upon its new career, some of those prophets had opportunity to witness the honors paid by princes, and the more heartfelt and more grateful tribute of their people, to that other simple-mannered American—ex-general, ex-President—who had borne his patient and heroic part in bringing their prophecies to naught.

Certainly during all these years the people of these States have made many efforts to improve their fundamental laws.   Up to the year 1860, thirty-four States in all had been admitted into the Union.   In that year there were only five States in which the constitutions under which they came into the Union still remained in force without change, namely, Texas, Wisconsin, California, Oregon, and Minnesota.   But these constitutions were only from three to fifteen years old, bearing date respectively in 1845, 1848, 1849, and 1857.   In several other States — Alabama, Oregon, Connecticut, Maine, Massachusetts, Missouri, and North Carolina,—though the constitutions first adopted had not been superseded, all had been more or less amended ; that of Missouri, for example, seven times, and those of Connecticut, Maine, and Massachusetts, eight times respectively. In each of the other twenty-two States at least two distinct constitutions, besides many amendments at various dates, had been in force up to 1860. The whole number of complete constitutions promulgated in those thirty-four States, up to the year 1860, was sixty-nine, besides one hundred and one different sets of amendments. The number of new or completely revised constitutions adopted since 1860—the number of States having since then increased to thirty-eight—is thirty-five, or an average of nearly one for each State during a quarter of a century. This includes, however, the first constitutions adopted for Colorado, Nebraska, and Nevada, admitted since 1860, and also the new or revised constitutions framed in eleven Southern States—Alabama, Arkansas, Florida, Georgia, Louisiana, Maryland, Missouri, South Carolina, Texas, Virginia, and West Virginia—during or immediately after the war, but which were in every case subsequently replaced by new ones, adopted in 1867 or later, and ratified by popular vote. The number of amendments adopted since 1860, treating whatever was adopted at one time as one amendment, though often containing several articles, has been, as near as I can ascertain, one hundred and fourteen in all. In other words, the total number of distinct constitutions, either newly adopted or completely revised, which have been promulgated in these thirty-eight States

in the one hundred and ten years since the Declaration of
Independence, has been one hundred and four, and to
those several constitutions two hundred and fourteen
partial amendments have been adopted at different times,
some of less and some of greater importance.

But it is also true that during the same period many
constitutional amendments, and some revised constitutions, have been submitted to the people in various
States, either by their Legislatures or by conventions,
which have been rejected by the popular vote ; of which
a notable instance occurred in your own State of New
York in 1869. During the last ten years twenty-eight
amendments, in seventeen States, and six complete or
revised constitutions, submitted to popular vote, have
been rejected.

These statistics have a certain interest, I think, in the
light of the statement already quoted from Sir Henry
Maine—that social necessities and social opinion are
always more or less in advance of Law, and that the
greater or less happiness of a people depends upon the
degree of promptitude with which the gulf between them
is narrowed. That statement applies, of course, even
more strongly to the current changes in statutory law,
which so much more largely and immediately reflect the
movements of public opinion than do changes in the
organic law.

But it is a trite saying that change is not necessarily im-
provement. Whether the changes thus made in the organic law of these States, while undoubtedly the result
of changes in public opinion, and in real or supposed

social necessities, have been wisely made, is not a question of figures, or of averages, but of substance, the complete answer to which time alone can give.

In connection with these changes, may be noted the action taken from time to time with reference to their submission to a direct popular vote for approval or rejection. This has not always taken place. Judge Jameson, in his valuable treatise on Constitutional Conventions, published in 1873, discusses this topic both with reference to the theory of our institutions, and as a matter of historical precedent. Referring to that work (Chapter 7) for details, I may give in brief the results of his historical inquiries.

It appears that up to 1873 one hundred and fifty-two conventions in all had been held in the United States for the purpose of framing, revising, or ratifying constitutions or parts of constitutions, either for the Union or for States now members thereof ; including in that number twenty-eight conventions called simply to ratify propositions made by other conventions or bodies having analogous functions—such as the several State conventions which ratified the Federal Constitution,—and six others which proved abortive, such as various meetings of the Councils of Censors of Pennsylvania and of Vermont, and the Rhode Island Convention of 1834. Of the remaining one hundred and eighteen conventions, properly speaking, seventy-eight submitted the fruit of their labors to the people, including the convention which framed the Federal Constitution, and forty did not. But the significance of these figures can be got at only by considering their distribution in point of time.

Of the first constitutions formed by the colonies during the Revolution, only one was submitted to popular vote, namely, the Massachusetts Constitution of 1780. The Rhode Island Charter of 1663 was not superseded or amended at all till 1842, and the Connecticut Constitution of 1776, so called, which was framed and promulgated by the Governor and Council, was little more than a declaration of independence of Great Britain,—the Charter of 1662 remaining substantially in force until the Connecticut Constitution of 1818 was adopted. The other ten first constitutions of the original colonies, from that of New Hampshire in 1775, to that of Vermont in 1777, were promulgated by the " Congresses " or conventions which framed them, and were accepted by the people. This resulted largely, no doubt, from the disturbed condition of the country while the war was going on, and the uncertainty of its issue. But all first constitutions which have been framed by conventions for States admitted into the Union since the Revolution, from that of Kentucky in 1792 to that of Colorado in 1876, appear to have been submitted to a vote of the people.

X Down to 1873, seventy-nine Revising Conventions had been held in all, including under that term as well those which only proposed amendments, as those which framed complete constitutions. Of these fifty submitted their labors to the popular vote, from that of Massachusetts in 1779 to that of Texas in 1861. The work of the remaining twenty-nine conventions took effect without popular ratification, from that of South Carolina in 1777 to that of Texas in 1866.

This subject, and the reasons for the diverse action so taken during so long a period, are discussed with interesting detail by Judge Jameson. His conclusion, that notwithstanding the numerous cases of non-submission, the theory of our institutions and the practice in peaceful times require a popular ratification, is confirmed by the provisions now in force in the States generally for the amendment and revision of their constitutions.

A summary of these existing provisions is given in the recent and valuable work of Mr. Stimson, entitled "American Statute Law." It may be said in general, that two distinct modes of amending State constitutions are provided for, as to which respectively numerous and varying checks and restrictions are imposed. One of these, I need hardly say, is by amendment proposed by the Legislature, the other by amendment or revision of the constitution, in part or whole, by a convention called for the purpose. Provision is made for both these modes in the constitutions of nearly all of the States; of which Article XIII of the present constitution of New York is an example.

As to the former method, by amendments originating with the Legislature, in most of the States either House may originate them. But in Vermont they can be proposed by the Senate alone, and that only once in ten years; in Connecticut, by the House alone. For their adoption is required, in some States, the vote of a majority, in others of three fifths, in others of two thirds of all the members-elect in each House. In only one State is the vote of a majority of the members present in each

House sufficient. In some, they must be adopted by two successive Legislatures: either by a majority of the members-elect of each House, or by a majority of one Legislature and two thirds of the next, or by three fifths of one and two thirds of the next, or by two thirds of one Legislature and three fourths of the next.

In two States amendments cannot be proposed to more than one article in any one session of the Legislature; in two not more than three amendments can be submitted at the same election; in another, while an amendment approved by one Legislature awaits the action of the next, no other amendment can be proposed. In New Jersey and Pennsylvania amendments cannot be submitted to the people oftener than once in five years, in Tennessee not oftener than once in six years. In Indiana, while an amendment approved by one Legislature awaits the action of its successor, no other can be proposed; and in fourteen States, if two or more amendments are submitted at the same time, they must be separately submitted. Such restrictions indicate a wholesome fear of hasty action by an accidental majority.

But after the supposed will of the people has been thus expressed by their representatives, it is required in thirty-five States that amendments so adopted by the Legislature must be ratified by a vote of the people at the next election before they can take effect; and in one of these (Rhode Island) they must be again ratified by two thirds of the members of each House of the next Legislature elected after the popular ratification. In Delaware, amendments adopted by the Legislature are not submitted to the people, but must be ratified by the next Legislature. In Kentucky and New Hampshire, the Legislature is not authorized to propose or adopt amendments, but may submit the question of holding a convention to the people; and in the latter State the sense of the people on that question is required to be taken in their town meetings at the end of every seven years.

So, as to the mode of amendment or revision by conventions, numerous precautions against hasty action are provided.

In twelve States, including New York, when a majority of the members-elect of each House—or in Nebraska when three fifths, and in other States when two thirds of such members—vote that such convention is necessary, the question is referred to the people. If the vote at the next election (in Kentucky at two successive elections) is in favor of holding a convention, the Legislature is required in twenty-five States to provide therefor, the delegates in all cases to be elected by the people. In some States the Legislature is required at stated intervals to submit to the people the question of holding such a convention, as in New Hampshire, every seven years; in Iowa, every ten years; in Michigan, every sixteen years; in New York, Ohio, Maryland, and Virginia, every twenty years.

In some States, as in Missouri, the constitution expressly denies to the Legislature any power to call such conventions except in the manner and under the conditions therein prescribed. Important questions have arisen, and may again arise in the absence of such provisions, as to the extent of legislative powers in that regard. Of this an illustration occurred in New York in 1820, when a bill passed both Houses, by which a constitutional convention was to be called without referring the question to the people in the first instance, the amended constitution of 1777, then in force, containing no provision on that subject. This bill was sent to the Council of Revision, of which Governor Clinton, Chancellor Kent, and the Judges of the Supreme Court were members, and a majority of the Council vetoed the bill, on the single ground that it did not propose to submit to the people the question of holding a convention, while it did contemplate submitting to them an amended constitution, as a whole, to be adopted or rejected *in toto*, without discrimination. This veto message is given in full as an appendix to Judge Jameson's work, and it can hardly be doubted that the views presented in that very able paper, written by Chancellor Kent, have had much to do with the provisions since adopted in this and other States on that subject.

It appears, I think, from the facts thus imperfectly summarized, that the people of these States, while making careful provision for the amendment of their organic law from time to time, thus " narrowing the gulf" between existing law and the social opinion and social necessities which constantly tend to go beyond it, have constantly sought to guard against hasty action as well on their own part as on that of their representatives. However different in detail, all such checks and restrictions indicate a settled purpose that, in the language of Chancellor Kent, in the veto message just mentioned, " time shall be given for mature deliberation upon questions arising upon the constitution, which are always momentous in their nature, and calculated to affect not the present generation alone, but their distant posterity." They are obstacles, as Mr. James Russell Lowell has well said in his admirable address on Democracy, " not in the way of the people's will, but of their whim." And if these details have been wearisome, you may perhaps find excuse for them in the reflection, that as the crucial test of human character is that habit of self-control which secures the ascendency of reason over passion and impulse, so there is no augury of the fate of popular institutions more important than that drawn from the limitations voluntarily imposed by a free people upon their own action.

Our American system of government is proverbially one of " checks and balances." This is true both of the State and the Federal Constitution, though necessarily of somewhat different application to each. Von Holst, in his History of the Federal Constitution, seems to consider such features in that instrument as the result alone of concessions and compromises between conflicting State interests, compelled by the circumstances of the time, and yielded only as the alternative " to the certain ruin consequent upon a continuation of the old confederation." Conceding this as to questions which arose between the States, it does not explain the distribution and limitations of power in State constitutions adopted before that crisis arose, as well as ever since. And however true it may be, as Von Holst says, that " the historical

fact is that the (Federal) Constitution was extorted from
the grinding necessity of a reluctant people," and that it
"was the living expression of the actual circumstances of
the time,"—whatever food for thought we may find in his
sharp criticisms of the "unconditional admiration" of
Americans for that instrument, and of what he describes
as "the self-complacency and pride of a people who es-
teem themselves special objects of the care of the Ruler
of the Universe,"—yet the fact remains that the people
of these States, while holding to their belief in a Divine
Providence controlling the affairs of men and the events
of history, have also constantly imposed restrictions
upon their own action as well as upon that of their
chosen representatives and public servants.

In mentioning some of the more recent changes in
American State constitutions, you will permit me to repeat that I do not attempt to enumerate all that are important, much less to instruct you as to their significance;
but only to suggest some inquiries which might be profitably followed up.

The most casual examination of the changes made in
those instruments during the last forty or fifty years,
gives plain indications not only that new questions have
arisen and new political problems presented themselves,
but that new methods have been adopted in the organic
laws of many States for meeting them.

None are more important than those which relate to
the qualifications for exercising the right of suffrage,—
the broad foundation upon which the whole frame-work
of popular government rests. None are more significant

of the vast changes which have taken place alike in public opinion and in the *status* of great numbers of the people of this country.

The enfranchisement of the colored race in the Southern States, their equal right to the protection of the law, and their exemption from discrimination by any State in the exercise of the elective franchise on account of race, color, or previous condition of servitude, were direct consequences of the civil war. But they were brought about by the 13th, 14th, and 15th Amendments of the Constitution of the United States and the Federal Statutes enacted in pursuance thereof, and not, in the first instance, by changes in State constitutions. These events, therefore, while of unspeakable importance to the future of the whole country, and at once imposing new limitations upon, and giving a new direction to, constititutional and statutory legislation by the States, are not within the scope of these observations. But they have resulted in action by the people of the several States, which indicates how radical was the political revolution thus accomplished, and the extent to which its results have been accepted.

In the cases of Minor *vs.* Happersett, 21 Wallace, 178, decided in 1874, and United States *vs.* Reese, 92 U. S., 217, and United States *vs.* Cruikshank, 92 U. S., 555–6, decided in 1875, the United States Supreme Court held that the right of suffrage in any State is not a necessary attribute of national citizenship, nor was that right conferred upon any one either by the Constitution of the United States as originally adopted, or by the 14th or

15th Amendment thereto,—the adoption of which respectively was proclaimed on July 28, 1868, and March 30, 1870. In other words, that court held that the right to vote in the United States comes from the States, though the right to be exempted from discrimination in the exercise of the elective franchise, on account of race, color, or previous condition of servitude, is secured to all citizens of the United States, by the 15th Amendment. Subject to that restriction it remained for the States respectively to determine what should be the qualification for suffrage; and the answer to that question furnished by the constitutions adopted or amended since the civil war is pertinent to this inquiry.

In 1860 the institution of slavery existed in fifteen States—in all which, at that date, the right of suffrage was confined to free white male citizens, otherwise qualified. In three of these States—Maryland, Delaware, and Kentucky—that provision still remains in the constitution. In the constitutions now in force in the other twelve, the word "white" no longer appears in that connection, nor is it found in that of the new State of West Virginia. Of the remaining twenty-two States, the constitutions now in force in Ohio, Kansas and Oregon alone still retain the word "white," in describing the qualifications of electors. I am speaking, of course, simply of existing provisions in State constitutions, without reference to the effect of the Federal constitution as amended.

But we find other new provisions in the constitutions of the former slave States, pertinent to this head, though not directly relating to the right of suffrage. Eleven of them—Alabama, 1875 ; Arkansas, 1874 ; Florida, 1868 ; Georgia, 1877 ; Louisiana, 1868 ; Mississippi, 1868 ; Missouri, 1865 and 1875 ; North Carolina, 1876 ; South Carolina, 1868 ; Tennessee, 1870 ; Virginia, 1870—now expressly prohibit slavery or involuntary servitude except for crime. In view of the 13th Amendment to the Federal constitution all such prohibitions of slavery must be taken as inserted in State constitutions *ex industria*. The Maryland constitution of 1867 prohibits the re-establishment of slavery, but claims compensation from the United States for its abolition. The Delaware constitution of 1831, though amended in 1875, does not mention the subject. The Kentucky constitution of 1850, which recognized slavery and prohibited emancipation without full compensation, remains unchanged ; propositions to hold a constitutional convention, submitted to the people in 1874, and again in 1883, having both been rejected by large majorities. The Texas constitution of 1876 does not in terms prohibit slavery, but confers the right of suffrage upon every adult citizen of the United States possessing certain other qualifications, among which race or color is not included.

It may also be observed that in thirteen of the remaining States—Vermont (1793), Rhode Island (1842), Ohio (1851), Wisconsin (1848), Minnesota (1857), Indiana (1851), Michigan (1850), Iowa (1857), Kansas (1859), Nebraska (1866), California (1849), Nevada (1864), Colorado (1876) —slavery is expressly prohibited by the constitution ; but in all these, except Nebraska, Nevada, and Colorado, such provisions antedate the civil war ; that of Vermont,

for example, being found in its original constitution of
1793.

In connection with these may also be noted such provisions as that in Georgia that the social status of the
citizen shall never be the subject of legislation; in Virginia, South Carolina, Alabama, and Florida, that all
citizens of the State possess equal civil rights and political rights and public privileges; in West Virginia, that
every citizen is entitled to equal representation in the
government; in Arkansas, that no citizen shall be de-
prived of any right or exempted from any duty on
account of race or color; in Maryland, that no person
shall be incompetent as a witness on account of race or
color, unless hereafter so declared by Act of the General
Assembly; in Mississippi, that the right of all citizens to
travel on all public conveyances shall not be infringed;
and in North Carolina and Tennessee, prohibiting the
intermarriage of white persons with negroes or mulat-
toes, or their cohabitation as husband and wife,—which
last is in twelve other States prohibited by statute.

✓ Pertinent here also, though properly falling under the
head of education, are the constitutional provisions in
West Virginia, North Carolina, Tennessee, Missouri,
Texas, Georgia, and Alabama, that white and colored
children shall be taught in separate public schools. On
the other hand, the Louisiana constitution of 1868 forbids
separate schools for any race exclusively; and those of
South Carolina and Colorado provide expressly that the
public schools shall be open to all children without distinction of race or color.

But a study of American State constitutions shows that questions of race and color are not the only ones which have been mooted in respect of the right of suffrage or of holding office. If time permitted, it would be interesting to note the various changes which have been made in respect of property and educational qualifications ; and in respect of the prior residence required for voters, and the extension of the suffrage to persons not citizens of the United States ; also, how far the agitation in favor of permitting women to vote and hold office has impressed itself upon the organic law. I can barely allude to these important heads.

As to a property qualification, it must suffice to say that whereas this was formerly required in many States, —as, among others, in Maryland until 1810, in Massachusetts until 1822, in New York until 1826, in New Jersey until 1844, in Connecticut until 1845, in Virginia until 1850, in North Carolina until 1865, and in Pennsylvania until 1873,—Rhode Island is, I believe, the only State now requiring an elector to own property, though in several he must have paid such taxes as required of him, or a poll-tax if required by law. On the other hand, the constitutions of Minnesota, Kansas, North Carolina, Arkansas, California, Alabama, and Mississippi, now provide that there shall be no property qualification for the right of suffrage. In 1882, the payment of a capitation tax as a pre-requisite for voting was abolished in Virginia, and an amendment was adopted in South Carolina forbidding the General Assembly ever to pass any law that will deprive any of the citizens of that

State of the right of suffrage except on due conviction of treason, murder, burglary, larceny, perjury, forgery, or other infamous crime, or duelling. The Texas constitution of 1876 contains an important provision, to the effect that while all qualified electors, who during the six months next preceding a municipal election have resided in the municipality, may vote for all elective officers thereof, none but those who pay taxes on property in such municipality may vote in any election to determine expenditure of money or assumption of debt. The significance, and I venture to add the wisdom, of this provision require no comment.

A provision similar in principle was contained in the very important amendment proposed as Article XVII to the constitution of New York, and which passed the Legislature of 1877, but failed in that of 1878. That amendment excited the liveliest interest in other States, for it dealt with one of the gravest problems now before the people of this nation,—the honest, economical, and efficient administration of municipal governments.

In many States every male of foreign birth aged twenty-one, who has declared his intention to become a citizen according to the United States naturalization laws, not less than a prescribed time before the election, is permitted to vote,—the time so prescribed varying from thirty days to one year. In every State a certain period of residence in the State prior to the election is required, —in two by statutes, in the rest by the constitution,—the time so prescribed varying from sixty days to two years, but one year being the prescribed period in a large majority of the States. In many States the voter must also have resided in the voting district for a period varying from ten days to one year.

The organic law of some States, and the amendments proposed in others, show the activity of the modern movement in favor of permitting women to vote and hold office. Every State constitution now in force specifies that the elective franchise is confined to males. But the constitution of Wisconsin authorizes the Legislature to extend the right of suffrage to persons not enumerated therein as electors, such law to take effect if approved by a majority of the votes cast at a general election. By the Colorado constitution of 1876 the Legislature was required at its first session, and authorized thereafter, to enact laws extending the right of suffrage to women of lawful age, otherwise qualified, the same to take effect if approved by a majority of electors at a general election. Such a law was passed, and in October, 1877, was submitted to popular vote, but was rejected by 14,000 to 7,400. Similar amendments have since then failed or been rejected in other States: in the Indiana Legislature of 1883, after passing that of 1882, and by popular vote in Nebraska in 1882, and in Oregon in 1884. On the other hand, women are now permitted to vote, in all respects like men, in the Territories of Washington, Wyoming, and Utah.

But in respect of educational matters such propositions have met with more favor. The constitution of Kansas prescribes that the Legislature, in providing for the formation and regulation of schools, shall make no distinction between the rights of males and females. Those of Minnesota and Colorado provide that women aged twenty-one may vote at any election of school officers or upon any measure relating to schools, and may hold any office pertaining solely to the management .hereof : and a like provision as to holding such office is found in the constitutions.of Pennsylvania and Louisiana.

The several changes already mentioned plainly mark the constant tendency towards putting completely into practice that theory of government so tersely expressed by Mr. Lowell in his address on Democracy, already mentioned :

" The democratic theory is that those constitutions are likely to prove the steadiest which have the broadest base, that the right to vote makes a safety-valve of every voter, and that the best way of teaching a man how to vote is to give him the chance of practice."

Nevertheless, the tendency has not always been absolutely uniform, nor has the theory of universal suffrage been maintained without exception. The race questions which have excited so much feeling on the Pacific coast, and which have become not only prominent in the legislation of those States, but also matters of national concern, are familiar to us all.

The Oregon constitution of 1857, still in force, provided that no Chinaman, not previously a resident of Oregon, should ever hold any real estate or mining claim, or work any mining claim therein, and that the Legislature should provide by law, in the most effective manner, for carrying out this provision.

The first constitution of California, in 1849, while confining the right of suffrage to white male citizens of the United States, made no other distinction of race. But the constitution of 1879 expressly withholds the right of suffrage from natives of China, in company with idiots, insane persons, and convicted felons; and the nineteenth article of that constitution is devoted entirely to that people. All corporations existing or to be formed under the State laws are forbidden directly or indirectly to employ any Chinese or Mongolian in any capacity. No Chinamen may be employed on any public work, except in punishment for crime. Penalties must be prescribed by law for the punishment of all companies, domestic or foreign, for the importation of Coolie labor, and the Legislature is required to delegate to municipalities all necessary power for the removal of Chinese from their limits, or their restriction to prescribed localities, and also to punish the introduction of Chinese into the State for the future. In Nevada, at the general election in 1880, constitutional amendments concerning suffrage and holding office, striking out the word " white " and forbidding discrimination on account of color and previous condition of servitude, were adopted by more than 14,000 votes against 600; while an amendment removing the existing prohibition against Chinese immigration was voted down by 17,259 votes to 183.

A different class of restrictions, present or prospective, upon the right of suffrage, appears in the constitution of four States—namely, an educational qualification. In Connecticut, by an amendment adopted in 1855, no

person can be admitted as an elector who is not able
to read any article of the constitution or any section
of the statutes of the State. In Massachusetts, an
amendment adopted in 1857 denies the right to vote
or hold office to any one who is not able to read
the constitution in the English language and to write
his name, saving persons already entitled to vote, or
physically disabled. The Florida constitution of 1868
required the Legislature to enact laws requiring educational qualifications for electors after the year 1880, saving all persons previously entitled to vote; and the
Colorado constitution of 1876 authorized the General
Assembly to prescribe by law after the year 1890 an educational qualification for electors with the like saving.
But the Alabama constitution of 1875 prohibits any educational or property qualification for suffrage or office, in
the same paragraph which forbids discrimination on
account of race, color, or previous condition of servitude;
and the Mississippi constitution of 1878 contains a similar prohibition in immediate connection with the prohibition of slavery.

This contrast between the provisions which require,
and those which, under very different circumstances,
forbid, an educational qualification for suffrage, is significant at once of the greatest danger and the greatest
dilemma which American institutions are forced to meet.
Such a requirement is but the complement of those declarations found in many State constitutions, that without
a general diffusion of knowledge and intelligence our
liberties cannot be preserved, and of those provisions

for the free education of all citizens which are found in almost all of them, and in pursuance of which such lavish provision has been made both by the Federal government and by the States themselves.

Upon that foundation, the base of the political edifice can not, indeed, be laid too broad. But, that condition disregarded—those foundations undermined and permitted to sink into the quagmire of popular ignorance—the time can not be far distant, as time is reckoned in the life of nations, when that edifice, once so fair and stately, shall be engulfed.

One other class of recent enactments made or proposed with reference to the exercise of that right, calls for brief mention,—namely, those which look to what is called minority representation.

The Illinois constitution of 1870 provides for the election of three representatives in each senatorial district, and allows each voter to cast three votes for one candidate, or to distribute his votes or fractions thereof among the candidates, as he may see fit. The same constitution permits shareholders, at corporate elections, to cumulate all their votes on one candidate, or distribute them among as many candidates as they may see fit. Like provisions concerning corporate elections have been adopted since 1870 in the States of Pennsylvania, Nebraska, West Virginia, Missouri, and California.

The Pennsylvania constitution of 1873 also directs that in elections at which two or more supreme judges, or two or more designated county officers, are to be chosen, each elector shall vote for only one of two, or two of three, candidates.   But in Ohio, in 1874, an amendment, separately submitted, which provided for minority representation in elections for three or more supreme and circuit judges, was rejected by a great majority.   The amendment to the constitution of New York, already mentioned, which passed the Legislature of 1877, but failed in that of 1878, authorized provision to be made by law for giving to minorities a proportionate share of representation in city boards.

Other details of constitutional changes in respect to voting and holding office might be mentioned, but I can detain you no longer upon this subject.   The further and important inquiry,—to what extent and in what manner such constitutional provisions are made effective by statutes and by that public opinion which gives its ultimate vitality and value to all legislation, is quite beyond the limits or purpose of these remarks.

Another class of notable changes in State constitutions, consists of those restrictions upon the law-making power, the frequency and extent of which have so greatly increased of late years.

It would be both tedious and useless to enumerate the successive steps in this direction or the particulars of such restrictions.   A comparison of constitutions in force fifty years ago, such as the constitution of Illinois adopted in 1818, of Missouri in 1820, or of New York in 1821, with the present constitution of Illinois adopted in 1870, of Pennsylvania in 1873, of Missouri in 1875 and California in 1879, not to mention amendments or revisions in other States, shows how great the change has been.

For example, the Missouri constitution of 1820, including all amendments up to 1855, contained but three express restrictions upon the power of the General Assembly
to pass laws:—one relating to banks, another to slavery,
and a third prohibiting legislative divorces. Article IV
of the Missouri constitution of 1875, now in force, contains fifty-six sections, more than half of which either
prohibit the enactment of laws upon designated subjects
or for designated purposes,or prescribe in detail the manner of enacting, amending, and repealing laws already in
force. Thirty-three of those sections relate to legislative proceedings. Eighteen of these are wholly new,
many of them copied from the Illinois and Pennsylvania
constitutions of 1870 and 1873 respectively, where they
first appeared ; and the remainder were first adopted in
Missouri in the constitution of 1865. The constitutions
of many other States contain restrictions of like character, though less numerous.

In many States the Legislature is now forbidden to pass
any local or special law in relation to certain designated
subjects, a complete list of which, as given in Mr. Stimson's compilation, exceeds sixty in number,—though all
of these are not found in any one constitution. A prohibition of this kind was added to the constitution of
New York in 1874, by which the enactment of private or
local bills in any of thirteen specified cases was forbidden.
In many States is forbidden the enactment of any
special, local or private law in any case for which provision has been (or in five States, may be) made by general law ; and in Missouri the question whether a general

law can be made applicable, is declared to be a judicial question, despite any legislative assertion to the contrary.

In twelve States the Legislature is forbidden to create any corporation whatever, municipalities included, except by general law, and in thirteen others, to create by special act any except municipal corporations or those to which no general law is applicable. In some States corporations can be created by special act only for municipal, charitable, or reformatory purposes. Such provisions are not intended to discourage the formation of private corporations. On the contrary, in all these States general laws exist under which they can be formed with great facility. Indeed, the defects in some of those statutes and their failure to provide safeguards against some, at least, of the very evils which they were intended to meet, might well suggest to legislators the question whether in avoiding the Scylla of special legislation, they have not been drawn into the Charybdis of franchises indiscriminately bestowed. Perhaps the time will come when recommendations such as have been urged by your own Railroad Commission will be acted on (N. Y. R. R. Comm'rs Report, 1884, p. 64), and the promoters of a new railroad will be required to furnish some better reason for its existence, and for their exercising the sovereign power of eminent domain, than the chance of forcing a company already established to buy them out,—or, failing that, the alternative of being sold out under foreclosure, pending a receivership.

But modern restrictions upon the law-making power relate to much more than the enactment of special or local laws. They include in some States stringent provi-

sions as to the manner in which bills must be introduced,
entitled, enacted, amended, or repealed ; restrictions upon
or prohibitions of the creation of State or municipal
indebtedness ; denials of power to grant or authorize
extra compensation to any State or municipal officer,
agent, or contractor ; prohibitions against the granting of
public money or loaning the public credit to any person
or corporation, and against the release of debts due to,
or liens held by, the State ; against appropriations in aid
of any church or religious denomination, or minister
thereof, or in aid of any benevolent or educational institution not wholly under the control of the State ; against
the levy of State or county taxes, or the authorizing of
municipal taxes, beyond a prescribed limit or percentage
upon the assessed value of the property taxed ; against
the contracting even of a permitted debt unless accom-
panied by prescribed provisions for its repayment within
a specified time ; and in some cases express prohibitions
against the assumption or payment by the State of certain designated claims, including, in five Southern States,
the assumption or payment of any debt or obligation in-
curred in aid of rebellion against the United States.   In
many States legislative sessions are restricted to a specified number of days, though in some the Legislatures are
permitted to sit longer at reduced rates of compensation.
In some, no bill introduced after a certain number of days
from the beginning of the session can become a law.   A
tendency to discourage frequent sessions is also shown by
the fact that within the last ten years, in at least six
States, annual sessions have been changed to biennial,

which a large majority of the State constitutions now
prescribe.

A novel restriction upon the Legislature in the matter
of appropriations was added to the Missouri constitution
in 1875. This provides (Art. IV, Sec. 43) that all State
revenue from every source shall go directly into the
treasury, and the General Assembly shall have no power
to divert the same or permit money to be drawn there-
from except in pursuance of regular appropriations made
by law. It is then prescribed that all appropriations of
money shall be made by the General Assembly in the
following order of priority: *first*, to pay all interest upon
the State debt falling due during its term of office; *second*,
two hundred and fifty thousand dollars annually for the
sinking fund; *third*, for free public-school purposes;
fourth, the cost of assessing and collecting the revenue;
fifth, the payment of the civil list; *sixth*, the support of
the eleemosynary institutions of the State; and *seventh*,
for the pay of the General Assembly, and such other
purposes, not prohibited by the constitution, as it may
deem necessary; and the General Assembly is forbidden
to appropriate money for any purpose until these appropriations have been made, in the order specified, or to
change the prescribed priority of any item.

These are some of the limitations imposed, of late
years, upon the law-making power. As to their wisdom,
I have nothing to say. The significant fact is, that they
are imposed by the people upon their chosen representatives as part of the organic law.

What conclusion are we to draw from such limitations?

It may be that the sceptic of popular institutions would point to them as proof that the people of these States, conscious of the decay of public virtue, have already come to distrust themselves in the persons of their representatives. But no such conclusion would follow, I think, upon a fair consideration either of the purpose or the effect of such constitutional provisions.

Restrictions upon the passage of special laws in respect of matters of merely local or individual concern, in cases to which general laws may be made applicable, are of manifest advantage to the community; not only on account of the great saving in time, labor, and expense of legislation thus accomplished, but for other reasons. They provide uniform methods of administration in local matters: which, under like circumstances, is obviously desirable, since general laws upon such subjects are likely to be enacted with more circumspection, and defects in their working are more likely to be observed and remedied, while unity and simplicity in the general body of administrative law is preserved. General and uniform laws, framed with due care and foresight, authorizing the formation of private corporations upon compliance with reasonable and prescribed conditions, while they promote and facilitate the aggregation and employment of capital in many enterprises of private and public benefit whose prosecution would often be needlessly impeded by the necessity of applying to the Legislature for a special charter, also prevent the obtaining of special privileges and exemptions without adequate return therefor to the community. And so of other restrictions upon the law-making power, already mentioned,—which may well be considered, not as evidencing a distrust of popular institutions, but rather as additional precautions taken by the people themselves against dangers confessedly inherent in them,—or rather, in human nature itself.

Fifty years ago, De Tocqueville, an ardent friend of popular institutions, pointed out that the greatest danger of the American republics proceeded from "the unlimited power of the majority, which," he adds, "may at some, future time urge the minorities to desperation, and oblige them to have recourse to physical force." In support of this, he cites both Hamilton and Jefferson,—the latter, as being "the most powerful advocate democracy has ever sent forth"; and quotes from a letter of Jefferson to Madison, in 1789, the following words:

"The executive power of our government is not the only, perhaps not even the principal, object of my solicitude. The tyranny of the Legislature is really the danger most to be feared and will continue to be so for many years to come."

Another class of comparatively recent provisions in State constitutions consists of positive enactments, such as we should hardly expect to find in the organic law.

Such are provisions fixing at specified sums the salaries of State officers; limiting the rate of interest, legal and conventional; exempting certain property from levy on execution; prescribing details of practice in the courts; constitutional enactments concerning the property of married women, which, in several States, provide, what is quite as effectively done by statute in others,—that the property of a woman held before marriage or acquired after her marriage by gift, grant, devise, or descent, shall remain absolutely her own. In Missouri, the reception of deposits by a bank in failing circumstances is declared a crime on the part of directors cognizant thereof, who are also made civilly liable for the same. The California constitution of 1879 prescribes eight hours as a legal day's work on all public works; and in terms creates, in favor of mechanics, material-men, and laborers, a lien upon the property on which they have furnished material or labor, though leaving the enforcement of such lien to the Legislature.

Numerous other illustrations of this tendency might be mentioned. Perhaps the most notable one is the adoption of what are known as prohibition amendments; as, in Kansas, in 1880, Iowa in 1882, Maine in 1884, and Rhode Island in 1886; while in other States like amendments are now being vigorously urged.

It would ill become me, on this occasion, to discuss the merits of such legislation. The only inquiry now suggested is,—why it should find a place in the constitution, especially since both State and Federal courts have upheld such statutes as constitutional under the police power of the States, and a prohibitory liquor law has been on the statute-books of Maine for many years past.

This inquiry is a very important one. It involves the true scope and office of the constitution itself. As to this, Judge Cooley says (Const. Lim., p. 3):

" In American constitutional law, the word constitution is

used in a restricted sense, as implying the written instrument agreed upon by the people of the Union, or of any one of the States, as the absolute rule of action and decision for all departments and officers of the government, in respect to all points covered by it, which must control until it shall be changed by the authority which established it, and in opposition to which any act or regulation of any such department or officer, or even of the people themselves, will be altogether void."

This is not the only function of a constitution under a free government. It fulfils a still more important office, in declaring those natural and fundamental rights of individuals for the security and common enjoyment of which governments are established. To the end that those rights may be so enjoyed and protected, such a constitution, or the laws enacted in pursuance thereof, may control their exercise by individuals ; and, to such extent as the common good shall require, may prescribe the mode of their enjoyment. But those rights are not derived from nor measured by the constitution. It does measure and limit the powers of the officers to whom is committed the duty of protecting and enforcing them ; and it is to this view of an American State constitution that the description above quoted applies.

In this sense a State constitution is properly called an organic law,—the fundamental law pursuant to which the State government is permanently organized and conducted. It is not a code, civil or penal ; and whatever tends to turn it into one, endangers its ultimate stability by exposing it to every gust of popular excitement or caprice. The difference between putting into a State constitution, and prescribing by a statute, a rule of conduct affecting individuals alone, is that the latter can be repealed by the next Legislature, while the former cannot. But to put into the constitution, *for that reason*, a rule which a statute would sufficiently prescribe, and which must be supplemented by a statute to make it effective, would be simply to take advantage of the greater permanency of the organic law in the interest of a majority —perhaps a merely apparent or temporary majority,—for a purpose quite foreign to the purpose of that instrument ; and might well argue a distrust, on the part of that majority, of their ability to maintain their ground in the convictions of the people. If this be the significance of constitutional provisions such as I have mentioned, it is not an encouraging sign. It would exemplify that tyranny of the majority which the friends, as well as the foes, of democratic institutions concede to be their greatest inherent danger.

Indeed, the experience of the good people of your own State shows, that even in respect of one of those fundamental rights already referred to, a constitutional guaranty may be safely dispensed with, so long as such right is declared and enforced by a statute, which is upheld by the general sentiment of the people. Neither the present nor any former constitution of the State of New York contains that prohibition of " unreasonable searches and seizures," and of the issue of search warrants except upon probable cause, supported by oath or affirmation, which is found in the constitution of every other American

State, and was adopted as the fourth amendment to the Federal Constitution. Such a declaration is found, however (in language identical with the amendment last mentioned), in the Bill of Rights, enacted *as a statute* in this State, in 1787 ; and is enforced by statutory requirements touching the issue and service of search warrants which yield in strictness to no others.

Other classes of novel and highly important provisions in American State constitutions consist of those which relate to private corporations and *quasi* public corporations, and also, in one State, to public warehouses. Of such provisions, those adopted in Illinois in 1870, Pennsylvania in 1873, Missouri in 1875, and California in 1879, furnish the most notable examples, though some are found in other States.

Of those relating to corporations, some, already noted, prohibit their creation except by general laws, subject to repeal or amendment ; others forbid the granting to them of exclusive privileges ; others limit their duration, and their power to hold real estate. Others prescribe specific rules for the conduct of corporate business, as in respect of the issue or increase of their stock or bonded indebtedness, or the manner of electing their officers, or the individual liability of stockholders for corporate debts.

Those relating to railroads and other carriers, and to public warehousemen, are even more significant of the vast development of our industrial civilization, the changes in means and modes of transportation, the enormous increase in the internal commerce of the nation, and the new problems which we are called upon to meet as well as the controversies to which they have given rise. The novelty, the vast importance, and the significance of the facts from which have resulted constitutional provisions like these, are thus forcibly stated in the opening paragraphs of Professor Hadley's very valuable work on Railroad Transportation.

On the fourth of July, 1828, Charles Carroll, last surviving signer of the Declaration of Independence, laid the first rail of the Baltimore and Ohio Railroad. One man's life formed the connecting link between the political revolution of the last century and the industrial revolution of the present. The second reaches wider and deeper than the first. Yet there are few who realize its full importance or who seriously try to understand it. A new system of commercial and social relations has arisen among us. . . . Of these changes the railroad is at once an instrument and an example. . . . No one symptom in business or in politics marks the direction of national activity so clearly as does the way in which the transportation system is organized and controlled.

Of these provisions, some define the relations of railroads to the State and its people, declaring them public highways and common carriers, and as such subject to legislative control ; others forbid discriminations in rates of freight or tolls, and the consolidation of parallel or competing lines, and prescribe conditions of consolidation in other cases ; others forbid any officer or agent of a railroad company to be interested in furnishing material or supplies to such company, or in the business of transportation as a common carrier of freight or passengers over its lines ; others forbid the granting of free passes to

State or municipal officers, or members of the General Assembly. In eight States every railroad is required by the constitution to permit any other railroad to cross or connect with its tracks, and in two States a Board of Railroad Commissioners is established by the constitution, while in others such boards have been created by statutes.

Such provisions, and others which I need not detail, sufficiently indicate the deep hold which these questions have taken upon the public mind, and the tendency of American legislation. They proclaim the advent of a new era, the emergence in the national life of new questions, vitally affecting every interest and every class. Von Holst remarks upon the curious fact that just as the United States are about to commence the second century of their life as an independent commonwealth, and as a republic,—

—at the same time, they evidently are entering upon a new phase of their political development. The era of buoyant youth is coming to a close ; ripe and sober manhood is to take its place.

Upon the just solution of such questions as these must depend, in part at least, the continuance of that life. No solution of them can be permanent or safe unless it be also just to every interest affected. To reach that solution will tax the highest resources of American statesmanship. Still more will it demand from the people themselves that moderation, that self-control, which shall resist alike the schemes of selfish interest, the arts of the demagogue, and the clamors of faction.

Shall we despair, then, because those questions are grave and difficult, and those interests apparently conflicting ?

Shall not this people, entering upon its ripe and sober manhood, looking back upon its lately turbulent youth, still hold to that faith which the laureate sang in earlier days ?—that faith in

Men, our brothers, men, the workers, ever reaping something new ;
That which they have done but earnest of the things that they shall do ?

Shall it not still be true of this land, that—

There the common sense of most shall hold a fretful realm in awe,
And the kindly earth shall slumber, lapt in universal law !

May I ask your indulgence for the mention of one other class of changes in American State constitutions, scarcely less important in their possible effect upon the tendency and the future of American institutions than those relating to the right of suffrage itself. I refer to the changes in the mode of appointing judges in many of the States.

How great those changes have been will best appear from a brief comparison of the constitutional provisions on this subject in force in the year 1800 with those which exist to-day.

In 1800 there were fifteen States in this Union, Kentucky and Tennessee having been admitted respectively in 1792 and 1796. In no one of those States were judges then elected by the people. In Delaware, they were appointed by the Governor alone ; in New Jersey, by the Council alone ; in seven States—Vermont, Rhode Island, North Carolina, South Carolina, Virginia, Tennessee, and

Georgia—by the Legislature. In the remaining six States, they were appointed by the Governor (in Pennsylvania then styled the President), but confirmed by some advisory body, which in Connecticut was the General Court, in Kentucky the Senate, and in Massachusetts, Maryland, Pennsylvania, and New York the Council. In twelve States, the judicial tenure of office was during good behavior. In New Jersey they were elected by the Council for seven years; in Vermont by the Legislature in joint committee, annually; while in Georgia the judges of the Supreme Court were appointed by the Legislature for three years, but those of the inferior courts during good behavior.

In 1886, the constitutional provisions on that subject are as follows :

In twenty-three States all judicial officers are elected by popular vote. In Connecticut, the judges of probate courts are so elected, and in Louisiana those of the district courts. In five, the judges are still elected by the Legislature, this mode of appointment never having been abandoned in Rhode Island, South Carolina, and Vermont, and the States of Virginia and Georgia having recently returned to it. In the remaining eight States the judges are appointed by the Governor, subject to confirmation either by the Council, as in Maine, Massachusetts, and New Hampshire, or by the Senate, as in Florida, Louisiana (as to Supreme judges only), Mississippi, and New Jersey; or by the General Assembly, as in Connecticut (since 1880), as to the judges of the Supreme and Superior Courts.

It would be a mistake, however, to suppose that during this entire period, and especially during recent years, the drift has always been in one direction. Such has been the fact, on the whole, as we have seen, in respect of the right of suffrage ; for the educational qualifications required in two States, and apparently contemplated in two more, not only do not conflict with the democratic theory of government, but are its most logical expression. They only put in practice the doctrine as to the necessity of popular education which nearly every State constitution declares, and upon which alone the taxes for the support of free public schools can be justified. But as to the mode of judicial appointments, the history of the changes made from time to time shows, I think, that the experiment is still in progress, that public opinion in regard to it has fluctuated and is still fluctuating, that in some States it has been abandoned, and that, even where it prevails, grave doubts exist as to its wisdom and its ultimate results.

May I still further presume upon your patience in briefly stating some facts from which these conclusions are drawn ?

The first departure from the old system was made in Georgia, in 1812, when an amendment to the constitution (made by the Legislature and not submitted to the people), provided that the justices of the inferior or county courts should be elected for a term of four years by the people of each county qualified to vote for representatives, the judges of the Superior Court being still elected by the Legislature. In 1816 Indiana was admitted into the Union, under a constitution providing a curiously mixed system of judicial appointments; the Supreme Court judges being appointed by the Governor and confirmed by the Senate, the presidents of the Circuit Courts being elected by the General Assembly on joint ballot, and the associate judges of the Circuit Courts elected by the people of the several counties—the terms of all judges being seven years.

No other change took place in any State until 1832, when Mississippi adopted her second constitution,—the first, adopted in 1817, having provided for the election of judges by the Legislature. Under this all judges were elected by the people, those of the Court of Errors and the Chancellor for six years, and the Circuit judges for four years. In 1835 Michigan was admitted, with a constitution under which the judges of the Supreme Court were nominated by the Governor and confirmed by the Senate, for seven years, the inferior judges being elected for four years by the people of each county.

In 1839, the constitution of Maine was amended by limiting all judicial terms to seven years, but the appointment of judges remained with the Governor and Council, as provided in its first constitution of 1820.

In May, 1846, a convention met in Iowa, which framed its first constitution, submitted to the people in August following, and ratified by a majority of about 450 votes out of 18,000. In June, 1846, a constitutional convention met in this city and framed a new constitution for New York, which was ratified in November, 1846, by a great majority. Both these constitutions made all judges elective by the people. In Iowa, the term of the Supreme Court judges was six years, that of the district judges four years. In New York, the judges of the Court of Errors and of the Supreme Court were all to be elected for eight years; the former at large, the latter by districts.

The example thus set was contagious. Within the next four years, eleven other States—Illinois, Wisconsin, Arkansas (in part), California, Pennsylvania, Missouri, Virginia, Alabama (in part), Connecticut (in part), Kentucky, and Michigan—adopted, in whole or in part, the method of popular election of judges; some by constitutional amendment, others in first or in revised constitutions—though in some with signs of hesitation. In Alabama and Arkansas the Chancellor and judges of the Supreme Court, and in Connecticut the judges of the Supreme and Superior courts, were still chosen by the Legislature. In Missouri, the first step, in 1848, was to change the terms of office of the Supreme and Circuit judges respectively from good behavior to twelve and eight years, still leaving their appointment to the Governor and Senate; but in 1850 another amendment to the constitution made all judges elective by the people for a term of six years.

Between 1850 and 1860 nine more States—Ohio, Indiana, Maryland, Louisiana, Tennessee, Maine, Minnesota, Oregon, and Kansas, the last three in first constitutions, the others by amendment or revision—adopted the elective system, in whole or in part; though in Maine only as to Probate judges, all others being still appointed by the Governor and confirmed by the Council.

In 1860, therefore, the plan of electing judges by the people had been introduced, to a greater or less extent, in twenty-four out of the thirty-four States then composing the Union; though in five of these,—Alabama, Arkansas, Connecticut, Georgia, and Maine,—the change affected only the judges of inferior courts; judges of the superior courts being still appointed in Maine by the Governor and Senate, and in the other four by the Legislature. But with the decade ending in 1860, this tendency seems to have reached its maximum, though its force was not yet spent. After 1860, the first constitutions of West Virginia, admitted in 1863, of Nevada in 1864, of Nebraska in 1866, and Colorado in 1876, made all judges elective; as did also the revised constitutions of Florida in 1865, of Texas in 1866, and of North Carolina in 1868.

But other changes have taken place since 1860 which indicate an opposite tendency,—either in the lengthening of judicial terms in States still retaining the elective system, or in the abandonment of that system by some States.

Thus, in New York, by the amendment of 1869, the judicial term (except in the county courts) was lengthened from eight to fourteen years; though at the same election a separate proposition to return to the former mode of appointment, by the Governor and Senate, was rejected by a large majority. In Pennsylvania, by the new constitution of 1873, the term was lengthened from fifteen to twenty-one years for Supreme judges, and from five to ten years for other judges. In Missouri, the term of Supreme Court judges was lengthened, in 1875, from six to ten years, and that of the judges of two intermediate appellate courts, more recently created, was made twelve years; in Ohio, where since 1851 the constitutional term was five years, the Legislature were authorized in 1883 to fix any term *not less* than five years; in California, the term of Supreme Court judges was changed from ten to twelve years; in Maryland, that of all judges from ten to fifteen years.

On the other hand, Virginia, by the new constitution of 1864, and also by that adopted in 1870 (amended in other respects in 1872, 1874 and 1876), has abandoned the system of popular election and returned to that of legislative election on joint ballot.

Louisiana, by the constitution of 1864, provided for the appointment of all judges by the Governor, and by that of 1868, for the appointment of the Supreme Court judges by the Governor and Senate, the district judges being again elected by the people. Mississippi, in 1868, abandoned the elective system entirely, all judges being now appointed by the Governor and confirmed by the Senate. By the Texas constitution of 1868, all judges were to be appointed by the Governor and Senate, though in 1876 that State returned to popular elections. Florida by the constitution of 1868, amended in other particulars in 1870 and 1875, abandoned the elective system, all judges being now appointed by the Governor and confirmed by the Senate. The Illinois constitution of 1870, while retaining the elective system generally, contains the anomalous provision that in Chicago, all justices of the peace shall be appointed by the Governor and confirmed by the Senate, but only upon the recommendation of a majority of the judges of the Circuit, Superior, and County courts; such justices elsewhere throughout the State being elected by the people. Maine in 1876 returned to the plan of appointing all judges by the Governor and Council; and Connecticut, by the amendment of 1880, provided that the judges of the Supreme and Superior courts should be nominated by the Governor, and confirmed by the General Assembly. And although during the ten years ending with November, 1886, revised constitutions have been adopted in three States, and numerous constitutional amendments on many different subjects in twenty-five States, no changes have been made in the mode of judicial appointment except those already mentioned. No State which had not already adopted the elective system has adopted it during that period.

It would be unbecoming, in this presence, to dwell upon the supreme importance, under popular institutions, of securing an independent as well as a learned and able judiciary. But I venture to think, in view of the facts already stated, that the best mode of securing that result is still an open question, and one which must continue to receive, as it unquestionably demands, the most anxious consideration. It is too much to hope that any mode of judicial appointment can be devised, human nature being what it is, which shall ensure the best possible results under all circumstances and in every case. As between the several modes of judicial appointment already mentioned, the real question is,—which of them, on the whole, will probably best endure the strain to which in some form or other it must be subjected, and which, sooner or later will surely find out where its weak-

ness is. If the discussion of that question were within
the scope of these observations, the most weighty reasons
could be given, as I think, in favor of the appointment
of all judicial officers by the Executive, subject to confirmation by a Council or Senate, to hold office during
good behavior; the ancient mode, which still prevails
under the Federal Constitution, and in eight States,
some of which, as we have seen, have in late years returned to it. Experience furnishes the weightiest of
those reasons. That system has not been a failure which
enriched modern jurisprudence with the labors of Kent,
of Marshall, of Story, and of Shaw. The dangers attend-
ing the election of judges by the Legislature were briefly
but forcibly referred to in the Address of Mr. Justice
Miller before your Association a few years ago. That
mode is generally conceded, I think, to be open to more
serious objections than either of the others.

But there is one consideration which seems to me of the
greatest moment, in reference to the election of judges by
popular vote; all the more, in view of that specious plea
sometimes urged in its favor, that since this is a representative popular government, and all who hold public office
are the servants of the people, judicial officers should be
elected in like manner with those whose functions are representative or executive. The obvious answer is, that not
only is a judicial office in no sense a representative one,
but just so far as its incumbent becomes, or is in danger
of becoming, the representative of any person, or measure,
or party, so far he becomes unfitted to hold it. But the
consideration to which I allude lies deeper than that.

Some of the most impressive observations made by De Tocqueville upon the probable future of American institutions relate to the functions of the judiciary, and especially to what he justly describes as " the immense political power " entrusted to American courts of justice, in the right, elsewhere unknown, of indirectly nullifying legislative action by denying its validity on constitutional grounds. But this power, as he points out, can be exercised only for the purposes of the case actually before the court ; and he adds :

If the judge had been empowered to contest the laws on the ground of theoretical generalities, if he had been enabled to open an attack or to pass a censure on the legislator, he would have played a prominent part in the political sphere ; and as the champion or the antagonist of a party, he would have arrayed the hostile passions of the nation in the conflict. . . . But the American judge is brought into the political arena independently of his own will. He only judges the law because he is obliged to judge a case.

I would gladly quote, if time permitted, his further comments upon this unique and most important feature of our system, but can only give his conclusion, as follows :

Within these limits, the power vested in the American courts of justice, of pronouncing a statute to be unconstitutional, forms one of the most powerful barriers which has ever been devised against the tyranny of political assemblies.

I need not remind you of the luminous and conclusive reasoning of Chief-Justice Marshall, in Marbury *vs.* Madi-

son, (1 Cranch, 70) in 1803, nor of the long list of subsequent decisions in State and Federal courts, affirming that
power in cases which practically attest the value set upon
it by our people. It may be doubted if any other feature
of our political system would not be sooner surrendered,
and with good reason.

But when De Tocqueville wrote those words, the Mississippi constitution of 1832 had not been promulgated.
The judges of whom he spoke were not nominees of
political parties, supported or opposed as such at comparatively short intervals, at the same election and on
the same ticket with candidates for the Legislature or
for Congress, nominated in like manner with themselves,
in the interest of the same political faith or the same
pending measures, but upon whose acts as legislators
they might at any moment be called judicially to pass.

It would be pertinent, I think, to an inquiry as to the
real drift or significance of such constitutional changes in
these States, to consider how far the election of judges
by popular vote may tend to weaken, even ultimately to
destroy, this most important barrier against the tyranny
of majorities, this obstacle (to repeat that felicitous
phrase), " not in the way of the people's will, but of their
whim." Such an inquiry would reach far beyond immediate or visible results. It is not answered by what hap-
pens under ordinary circumstances. Nobody doubts that
the American people desire pure and able judges, nor that
under ordinary circumstances they can and do elect them.
The honored names which have shone upon the roll of
your own judiciary during the past forty years, and which

still adorn it, and such tributes as that recently paid to
upright and able judges at the close of faithful service to
the people of your great city, demonstrate that.

But the strength and endurance of every political system and of every device for its security, like that of a
steamship or any other machine, must be measured by
that of its weakest part. It is the extraordinary strain,
not merely the ordinary one, which it must meet,—the
test of furious storms and heavy seas, as well as the gentle
wavelets of the placid bay, smiling in the sunshine of
popular content. In the political history of these States
many such storms have arisen, others even more furious
may still arise. The results of some of them are recorded
in those constitutional amendments which we have been
considering. Such were the controversies over the fugi-
tive slave law, over the validity of municipal and county
bonds issued in aid of railroads, over the granger laws, so-
called, within fifteen years past in Illinois, Iowa, and
Wisconsin, over the liquor-license laws in Ohio, over the
question of compensation to interests affected by prohibitory liquor laws, or by like constitutional amendments.

Is there no danger, under the system of popular election, that judges would be nominated, and their election
secured or defeated, not exclusively with reference to
their ability, their learning, or their purity, but because
they were supposed to represent or not to represent the
views of the political majority for the time being upon
any such controversy? I am afraid that history has already answered that question.

In Professor Hadley's important work on Railroad

Transportation, already mentioned, is thus narrated (p. 134), in part, the earlier history of the controversy over legislative control of railroad rates.

The first tangible results were reached in Illinois. The constitutional convention of 1870 made an important declaration concerning State control of rates, on the basis of which a law was passed, in 1871, establishing a system of maxima. This law was pronounced unconstitutional by Judge Lawrence. The result was, that he immediately afterward failed of re-election solely on this ground. The defeat of Judge Lawrence showed the true significance of the farmers' movement. They were concerned in securing what they felt to be their rights, and they were unwilling that any constitutional barriers should be made to defeat the popular will. They had reached the point where they regarded many of the forms of law as mere technicalities. They were dangerously near the point where revolutions begin. But they did not pass the point. The law of 1873 avoided the issue raised by Judge Lawrence against that of 1871. Instead of directly fixing maxima, it provided that rates must be reasonable, and then further provided for a commission to fix reasonable rates.

The merits of that controversy are quite foreign to my present purpose. It was finally determined, as to the question of constitutional power, by the United States Supreme Court, in 1877 ; but long before that decision was given, the effects of such legislation, especially in Wisconsin, were tested by experience. As Professor Hadley adds :

The very men who passed the law in 1874 hurriedly repealed it after two years' trial. In other States the laws either

were repealed, as in Iowa, or were sparingly and cautiously
enforced. By the time the Supreme Court published the
" Granger decisions " the fight had been settled, not by constitutional limitations, but by industrial ones.

Whatever other lessons events like these may teach,
surely they have an important bearing upon any inquiry
into the true significance of such constitutional changes
as those last mentioned. Such an inquiry would be interesting if it related only to the reasons which induced
their adoption. It becomes a much more momentous
question when it relates to the ultimate effect of such
changes upon the real independence of American judges.

Mr. President and Gentlemen :

The constitution of your Association, in enumerating
the objects for which it was formed, assigns the first place
to the cultivation of the science of Jurisprudence. It is
the glory of that science that it is concerned with living
human interests, with the rights and duties and mutual
relations, and therefore with the highest earthly interests,
of all civilized men. Its development not only keeps pace
with, but is essential to, the true progress of humanity. But
it is as true of this as of the sister sciences which deal with
inanimate nature, that its development can be attained
only in the use of scientific methods ; by patiently collecting the facts of human experience, under varying
conditions, by the careful comparison and classification
of those facts, and by deducing from them those general
rules and principles for the regulation of human conduct,

the knowledge and application of which distinguish the
scientific man from the sciolist, the jurist from the case-
lawyer. Its highest results are to be reached through
the study of comparative jurisprudence, increasingly
characteristic of our times. Surely there is no more in-
viting field for that study, none which promises a richer
harvest, than that which is offered to us in the laws and
constitutions of these American States,—one and yet
many, kindred and yet diverse, within whose busy bor-
ders are found representatives of every race, of every industrial interest, of every shade of human belief, every
stage of human thought. The existence, much more the
past labors, of your Association, and the important subjects which you have discussed, together with the activity
of similar Associations in many other States, afford gratify-
ing evidence that the American Bar is not unmindful of
its great opportunity.

To this great work it is the privilege of each one of
us in some measure to contribute ; if only, as I have to-
day attempted, by helping to hew out a few stones, which,
when fitly joined together by some master builder of our
profession, may be used towards erecting the edifice of
American Jurisprudence, of which this magnificent capi-
tol of your Empire State may well be a symbol. Founded
on the rock of justice and equal right, its massive walls
" four square to all the winds that blow," its portals open
to the humblest, while its spacious chambers worthily receive the greatest,—may that edifice forever stand, forever
grow, the abiding-place forever of Liberty and Law.